My Science Library

Animal Habitats

by Julie K. Lundgren

Science Content Editor:
Kristi Lew

Rourke
Educational Media

rourkeeducationalmedia.com

Science content editor: Kristi Lew

A former high school teacher with a background in biochemistry and more than 10 years of experience in cytogenetic laboratories, Kristi Lew specializes in taking complex scientific information and making it fun and interesting for scientists and non-scientists alike. She is the author of more than 20 science books for children and teachers.

www.rourkeeducationalmedia.com

Project Assistance: The author also thanks Riley, Sam and Steve Lundgren.

Photo credits: Cover © Paul S. Wolf, Damla AYZEREN; Cover logo frog © Eric Pohl, test tube © Sergey Lazarev; Page 4 © lavigne herve; Page 5 © Vittorio Bruno; Page 6 © Diana Cochran Johnson; Page 7 © Serg64; Page 8 © Eric Isselée; Page 9 © Henk Bentlage; Page 10 © JG Photo; Page 11 © Janelle Lugge; Page 12 © Strejman; Page 13 © Terence; Page 14 © Eric Isselée; Page 15 © Terry Reimink; Page 16 © Fiona Ayerst; Page 17 © Krzysztof Odziomek; Page 18 © Eric Gevaert; Page 19 © Eric Gevaert; ; Page 20 © Brian Balster; Page 21 © Morgan Lane Photography

Editor: Kelli Hicks

Cover and page design by Nicola Stratford, bdpublishing.com

Library of Congress Cataloging-in-Publication Data

Lundgren, Julie K.
 Animal habitats / Julie K. Lundgren.
    p. cm. -- (My science library)
 Includes bibliographical references and index.
 ISBN 978-1-61741-732-0 (Hard cover) (alk. paper)
 ISBN 978-1-61741-934-8 (Soft cover)
 1. Habitat (Ecology)--Juvenile literature. I. Title.
 QH541.14.L86 2012
 591.5--dc22
                         2011003867

Rourke Educational Media
Printed in the United States of America,
North Mankato, Minnesota

rourkeeducationalmedia.com

customerservice@rourkeeducationalmedia.com • PO Box 643328 Vero Beach, Florida 32964

Table of Contents

Hello, Habitat!

A **habitat** is where an animal lives.

Most black bears live in forests.

An octopus lives in the sea.

5

Animals need food, water, and **shelter** to live. They find these things in their habitat.

Some turtles need sunny places to warm themselves.

Some butterflies need flowers. They drink the sweet nectar.

7

Heaps of Habitats

Animals live in habitats on land and in water. Land habitats include forests, **grasslands**, and deserts.

Prairie dogs live in grasslands.

9

Deserts get very little rain.
They can be cold or hot.

The Arctic fox lives in a kind of cold desert called a tundra.

Some lizards live in hot deserts.

11

Tropical rainforests are warm and wet all year. These habitats are near the **equator.**

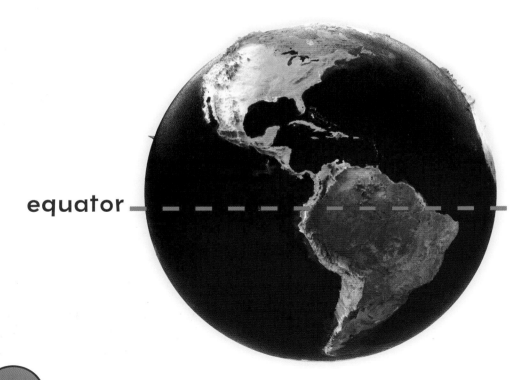

equator

Many kinds of monkeys live in the trees in tropical rainforests.

Oceans, lakes, and **wetlands** are water habitats.

You can find frogs and ducks in wetlands.

Oceans are salty water habitats. Most lakes are fresh water habitats.

Sharks patrol ocean waters looking for their next meal.

Freshwater pike live in many North American lakes.

17

Changing Habitats

People change habitats. These changes may hurt animals.

Oil spills can spoil water and land habitats.

Sometimes people cause big changes to habitats and then animals cannot find what they need.

Cutting down trees changes the forest habitat.

People must help take care of habitats.

SHOW What You Know

1. Can you name some land habitats?

2. What animals live in water habitats?

3. How can people care for animal habitats?

Glossary

equator (ee-KWAY-ter): an imaginary line around the middle of the Earth, halfway between the North and South Poles

grasslands (GRASS-landz): large areas of grassy land with few trees

habitat (HAB-uh-tat): a place an animal naturally lives

oceans (OH-shuhnz): salty bodies of water covering much of Earth

shelter (SHELL-ter): a place where an animal can be protected from danger and weather

tropical (TROP-uh-kuhl): warm and wet all through the year

wetlands (WET-landz): areas covered with shallow water and many kinds of water plants

Index

Websites

www.animalfactguide.com/

http://inaturalist.org/

www.kidsbegreen.org/

www.kidsbiology.com/animals-for-children.php

http://kids.nationalgeographic.com/kids/animals/

About the Author

Julie K. Lundgren grew up near Lake Superior where she liked to muck about in the woods, pick berries, and expand her rock collection. Her interests led her to a degree in biology. She lives in Minnesota with her family.